# Genius Lives

# Within

## Accessing our Birthright Power

# Margaret C. Pazant

 Reflections Publishing House

Margaret C. Pazant
P.O. Box 561453
Los Angeles, CA 90056
Marpazant@gmail.com
ISBN 978-0-9837231-9-6

Library of Congress Control Number 2013954071

*First Printing, July, 2014*

Editing by Martell Randolph-Ritter
and Paul Ritter
Cover Design by Sabrina Toston
Photography by Daniel Allen
Hair and Makeup by Angelle Clarke

Printed in the United States of America

Reflections Publishing House
PO Box 294, Inglewood, CA
reflectionspublishings.com

# CONTENTS

# ACKNOWLEDGMENT

To All my ancestors, Mom Hazel Pazant, Dad Roscoe Pazant Thank you. To my daughter, Jen Adcock I love you profoundly. Hazel Rivers, Ron Pazant and Carol Colas are the perfect siblings. Werner Erhardt, Sir James Robinson, Clyde Terry, John M. Hetrick, Regina Lewis and Ken Mandelbaum you are true visionaries. Reverend. Lisa Meggs thank you for recreating me. To the rest of you, and you know who you are I say "Gracias, Dumelong, Thank you, Nkosi, Merci, Asante Sana and Obrigado." Without our crossing paths I would have not had the opportunity to learn so many valuable and perfect lessons.

We Are One!

Margaret C. Pazant

# PREFACE

**W**hy now? When you come upon a thought and it is too soon or not fully developed, or it is not the right time to be received by group conscientiousness, the thought drifts away. If you come upon a thought and it has already occurred to everyone then its old news and nobody cares. When you come upon a thought at the perfect time in the perfect manner, then it is perfect. The outcome of that thought is perfect if you take the appropriate actions. After reading and re-reading James Allan's, *As a Man Thinketh*, I thought to myself, people have not really gotten his material. They have not gotten that our words create our world.

We live in the age of information and people have been reading religious books and spiritual information for decades and not getting the deeper meaning of these truths. I have just begun to receive them for myself on a very deep level and I have been searching and looking for answers for many, many years. I thought, "*what if I could communicate these deeper truths to others in a way that would have them get it for themselves?*" Then I thought to myself, *I can do that*. I *re*-member that I have always said that, as far back as I can remember, "*I can do that.*" Many times I said it to myself or to others when I saw, read, or heard something new or different. I'd say, "I can do that." I read books, took courses, and got certified and became a Master Life Coach. Every success I have had with clients and in my personal life is responsible for this book. Never in a million years did I think sitting on the floor in front of the television watching the Ed Sullivan show at six or seven years old with my family would over fifty years later have me write a book.

What I'm present to at this moment is that there is an opportunity for me to deliver this information *NOW;* in a way that people can get it. It's like there's an opening. There's a consciousness shift that is happening and it's been happening, and we're at a moment in time right NOW when a lot of people are ready to hear it. People have been waiting to hear it in a way that they can receive and understand it. I can say it to people in a way they can understand and they can truly get it; and that a lot of people can get it. This is what there is for me to do. I had the thought, took the actions on it and here is the result. And that is why the time to express this information is now.

We can only fulfill our deepest desires when we have a profound relationship with The Divine, Source, The Creator or whatever you choose to call her.

# A WORD ABOUT RESOURCES

This book is comprised of information designed to liberate and empower you from the inside out. It contains the very building blocks or foundations of your genius. Some of the chapters contain meditations, prayers, journaling and affirmations. Think of them as your personal GPS leading you to the riches of your Genius that Lives Within. From the opening pages you are guided along a journey created essentially by you. In other words, your unique and individual responses, observations and aware-ness about the material you encounter in this book create your specific journey. The book is designed to help you on your adventure. The resources provided to assist you are having you remember things long ago forgotten. They will provide a new awareness into the way you think, meditate, pray, journal and affirm. Here is a bit of information giving you the role of each resource in relationship to Genius Lives Within.

The first resource is **Meditation.** It is a pathway to attaining balance, inner peace and a real sense of calmness. Meditation is becoming aware of your breath and breathing as you silence your mind so as to be open to receiving inner guidance. By becoming balanced and centered you are no longer scattered and all over the place, just sit still, be quiet and listen for the voice of wisdom; Genius that Lives Within. Experiment until you find the meditation practice that suits you.

The second resource is **Prayer.** It will connect you to the Divine within in the form of contemplation. Prayer is the act of addressing your Higher Power in a direct conversation. It can be as simple as saying, "Thank you," or chanting Om, or calling on Jesus or Allah Akbar. You can recite any words of faith that you believe in, such as the Lord's Prayer, chants, the Psalms or other sacred words. If you are committed to receiving the full benefit of Genius Lives Within then meditation and prayer are essential. Prayer and meditation go hand in hand for a reason; the more consistent and committed you are to their practice, (the cause) the more immediate and lasting will be the result (the effect.)

The third resource is that of **Journaling.** When you write all that is important to you in your own handwriting, including your thoughts and dreams, this opens lines of direct communication with your inner Genius. Journaling is a mechanism which allows you to know what you are thinking and feeling at any time you choose. When you journal, no guesswork is required, no judging yourself or what you write, you are simply becoming aware of your thoughts and your true feelings and jotting them down.

Awareness of your thoughts and feelings is the first step on the road to managing them. Managing your thoughts and being taken over by your thoughts are not the same. When your thoughts take you over you are out of control. When you manage them you get to choose how things go and you are responsible for the outcome of your life. You are aware of what you are choosing and you own it, it is your choice. You have complete authority over the outcome of your actions.

The last resource is **Affirmations**. Creating in words will help to make manifest your intentions. They work to the degree you strength-en your belief system. The beauty of affirmations is that they have a powerful and positive effect immediately when you believe them. When you affirm and believe that which you are affirming is yours, it really is.

Whether you are using your own or those written by another, affirmations re-enforce and re-invigorate your commitment to manifesting that which you are affirming. It is causing you to say what it is that you desire. Remember, your words create your world.

Coupled with your openness and a desire to know your greatness, these resources will maximize your efforts and increase your understanding exponentially. You have the option of simply reading the material without using the resources provided and hoping for the best, but why would you? That's like the difference between taking a black and white photo of some-where out in nature and actually being somewhere out in nature instead. In the photo you may see the spectrum of light and shadow and see the different textures of the things depicted but actually being in nature would prove to be a much richer experience by far.

Genius Lives Within was designed to work as a tangible, living source of inner guidance and access founded upon the resources of prayer and meditation, journaling and affirmations.

Getting the most out of Genius Lives Within requires you to engage and interact with the material you read. This is not passive reading as if you were watching television or listening to the radio. Just as you instinctively utilize all of your senses to attune to the world without, using meditation and prayer, journaling and affirmations you attune to the Genius Living Within. Which would you prefer a photograph which can be destroyed or lost forever, or the live experience which cannot be taken away and becomes a part of you? You are created as a Spiritual Being having a human experience. And *always,* you get to choose the outcome of those experiences

## HONOR YOUR SPIRIT!

Genius Lives Within opens the door to total life altering success on every level, body, mind and soul.

Genius Lives Within focuses on leaving you aware, present, and responsible.

I urge you to take notes, practice, practice, practice, and follow the information held within.

**"Have faith, even as little as a mustard seed ~Luke 17:6 ~that this information will work for you and it will."**

# Begin To Work On Your Self-Confidence

Self-confidence is the foundation for all good. As you begin to grow in confidence, you develop a new level of assuredness and goodness multiplies in every area of your life.

Have strong and fundamental faith. Have an "I can do it attitude," and you will achieve your wildest dreams.

Know that wherever you are Source is with you.

Believe that today is the perfect day to live, love, learn and grow. Think about and ask yourself, what is my purpose in life? When you can answer this question through Divine Enlightenment you will know The Genius Lives Within.

# Foundation One

# Infinite Power

There is a World Within and a World Without. Each of these two worlds produces an outcome. The outcomes or results of these worlds account for our life as we know and experience it. When we realize that infinite power lives within us, we can be open to accepting that true genius lives within us.

## WORLD WITHIN

*Thought, Light, the Invisible, Feelings,*

*Aliveness, Strength, Compassion,*

*Power, Beauty, Love…*

*All of this is governed by the mind, which is more than just the brain.*

*The answer to every problem is the World Within.*

*The cause for every effect lives in the World Within.*

Within lives infinite wisdom and power. Unlimited supply is waiting to be created, developed and recognized by us. In other words, unlimited supply is waiting to be *given* to us. Once all of this is recognized within it will and must take form without. Genius lives in the World Within. When harmony is within, harmonious conditions exist without. Agreeable and uplifting surroundings show up *within* facilitating what we want in our lives *without*.

## WORLD WITHOUT

The World Without is a reflection of the World Within. We control the World Within, we cannot control the World Without, and hence, it is out of control. All of this is based on the natural laws of life. All laws relating to the world within, in particular laws regarding power and possessions, love, health and well-being are under our complete control. Everything is within, all love, all greatness, all power, all achievement, and all success. All of it is within, as well as the ability to control our thoughts.

| THE WORLD WITHIN gives… | THE WORLD WITHOUT creates... |
|---|---|
| *Harmony* | *Health* |
| *Alignment* | *Synchronizations* |
| *All our Needs are Met* | *Abundance* |
| *There is Optimism* | *Passion* |
| *There is Integrity* | *Workability* |

The World Without is a mirror of the state, conditions and consciousness of the World Within. Re-member a mirror always gives the reverse or opposite view. In the World Within we find wisdom; understanding the possibilities that exist for us. Doing this gives us the ability to make things manifest in the World Without. As we become aware of the wisdom within, we can claim our wisdom and from there we can create. The creation of courage, hope, enthusiasm, love, peace, joy and balance all come from within.

Dreams come from within. The fulfillment of our dreams and the manifestation of all our desires come from within. The blossoming of the seeds that are planted within must bear fruit without. This is a natural law, what we sow so shall we reap, some call this Karma. We build strength within, which gives harmony within, and manifest vitality and aliveness without.

When we have dis-empowered negative thoughts within they manifest distress, dis-ease, poverty, limitations, failure and loss without. Through dis-empowered thinking within, we radiate discord which attracts caustic, toxic, negative and dis-empowered circumstances without.

*Mindfulness makes a full man. A full man speaks with an open mind. And like a parachute, the mind works better when it is fully opened. This awareness is the key to unlock the door from conflict and strife as well as wholesome thoughts emerge."*

~Dr K Sri Dhammananda

## Food For Thought:

What do we mean when we speak of the World Without and its relationship to the World Within?

What is available to you when you live your life from within?

# Honoring Your Word

How do you become masterful at honoring yourself as your word and operating with a high level of integrity? First you need to understand what integrity means. Integrity comes from the word *integer*, meaning whole. In mathematics, an integer represents a whole number rather than a fraction. Integrity is wholeness and completeness, with nothing missing. When we actually live our lives from integrity we are living from that secret place that dwells within us. I like to call it *Honoring Your Spirit*. It is that unscathed point of completeness that lives within us. We produce results when we operate with integrity and honor ourselves as our word. These are the words you say to yourself and the words you say out loud. You do what you say and keep your promises and agreements. With practice, practice and more practice you can master honoring yourself as your word. Practice makes it possible to get as close to perfect as you can get.

What I mean by practice is repetition, doing that which you practice over and over again. Let's say you are committed to playing the piano. You start with learning the scales and then you practice playing them over and over, faster and faster until you have mastered them. Then you play a song, a sonata or a concerto. Then you are ready for your recital. Anything you do at the same time in the same manner for at least twenty-one days continuously becomes a habit. There's a famous joke that goes something like this, "How do you get to Carnegie Hall? Practice, practice, practice!"

## The Detox Period

*"When you refrain from habitual thoughts and behavior, the uncomfortable feelings will still be there. They don't magically disappear. Over the years I've come to call resting with the discomfort, "the detox period," because when you don't act on your habitual patterns, it's like giving up an addiction. You're left with feelings you were trying to escape. The practice is to make a wholehearted relationship with that."*

~ Pema Chodron

When I mentioned earlier about getting as close to perfect as you can get, I meant as perfect as we can get in a world where nothing is perfect and everything is perfect. When at the same time, the events of your life are working just the way you want them to, then you have given it your very best. There are laws or tools, and answers to the questions that you have and have not been asking. If you are willing to take on reading this book with faith, patience and discipline you will find the Genius that Lives Within and life will open up to you profoundly.

## Let's Dive Into the Conversation

Those that have get, those that don't have don't get. What does this statement say to you? You may have forgotten or you don't remember, but you do know. As you move forward through this book you will begin to remember. You will remember many things you may have forgotten. This book will remind you and you'll learn things that will support you in finding that "aha moment," that leads you to the Genius that Lives Within. Those that have get, those that don't have don't get. Said another way, the more you have the more you get. The less you have, the less you seem to get. Maybe you have been paying attention to the wrong things. Metaphorically speaking maybe you have been forcing the river instead of allowing it to flow. It is as if you are walking around with a fifty thousand dollar check in your pocket that you refuse to cash and you are broke. Remember, "I of myself can do nothing. It is the Spirit within who expresses and manifests as true success in my life."

You must become aware or conscious of your power. You can never become mindful of your power until you learn that all power is from within. This might be old news for some of you and new news for others, it makes no difference. You are here for a reason, so be open to the possibility that this is new news for you today. There is a World Within and a World Without. Each of these worlds produces outcomes. The results of these worlds give us our life as we know it.

*"Listen to me; be silent, and I will teach you wisdom"*

*~ Job 33:33(NLV)*

## Question to Ponder:

What does it mean to honor yourself as your word?

# Life Influenced By Integrity

What is meant by integrity? It means keeping your agreements and promises, including the ones you make to yourself. Integrity is doing what you said you were going to do. It is honoring yourself as your word even when no one is looking. This means doing what you said you were going to do and if you realize that you can't keep your promise or agreement, then communicating it to those who are expecting you to fulfill your promises right away. Let them know you won't be keeping your promise and letting them know what you are going to do instead. You do this before not keeping your promise, not after you missed the appointment.

Living a life influenced by integrity creates an environment of wholeness and completeness. When you are living a life of kept promises and fulfilled agreements things just work. You produce results and achieve success. When I speak of self-discipline I'm talking specifically about doing exactly what you said you were going to do to produce the results you desire even when you do not feel like doing it. Even, when no one is telling you what it is you have to do. You know what needs to get done. You know that you have to do it and you just do it. You do whatever it is that must be done while taking responsibility for it.

*A disciplined person always goes the extra mile.*
*Joyce Myer*

## Question to Ponder:

What does operating at a high level of integrity mean?

# Mind Is Always Creating

This is a big conversation. All of our thoughts are creative and we have the ability to create all that we desire. We can create the good, the bad and or the ugly if we choose to. We can build a bridge or tear down another person and cause them to cry. We have free will which allows us to use our creative energy however we choose. Everything that happens in life is a result of continuous thinking and your mental attitude at any given moment. The mind's attitude depends upon what the mind thinks about. The foundation of all power, every achievement, every result, the passion, and the things we accumulate in life depend on the way we think. We can never become masters of our power until we learn that all power comes from within. As said before, "This might be old news for some of you and it may be new news for others, it makes no difference." You are reading this material here and now for a reason. There are no accidents in life. Let it wash over you as if you are hearing it for the first time, and with this new awareness, be open to the new possibilities it inspires. We get to choose how our life goes. We have complete control over our lives and we have all that we need to succeed.

## Something to Think About:

If all thoughts are creative, what does that make you?

# Journal Response

A notebook or a journal is an important capture tool for all of your thoughts, insights and practices. It will make a difference if you journal while reading this book. Journaling is the practice of checking in with yourself at any given moment and jotting down your thoughts. It's a place to organize your thoughts, dreams, visions and ideas. Write anything you desire in your journal or just certain topics you wish to think deeper about. Place drawings, photographs, clippings, and scripture notes or write poetry in it. If an affirmation or prayer comes to mind, write it in your journal. Use your own personal journal or a notebook to capture what moves you during the day or anytime you have a thought you wish to remember. Use it to manage everything you want to refer to or hold on to in the future. It is your journal to be used for your personal growth and inspiration.

Write in your journal daily all that you are becoming aware of as you read and practice the information in this book. What are you thinking about? What is going through your mind as you sit in the silence? Are you thinking empowered thoughts, happy and uplifting thoughts, or dis-empowered, angry and confused thoughts? Remember to breathe, take nice deep breaths to get settled into the present moment before and after you begin writing in your journal.

*"We can never become masters of our power until we learn that all power comes from within." ~M.C. Pazant*

After you have finished reading the statement above, think about what it is saying then answer the following questions:

How do you hear this statement? Is it with resistance or with openness?

What emotions come up for you? How do you feel right now?

# Foundation Two

# Words Create Your World

Our words create our world. We have created a world of opinions, judgments and dis-empowered thoughts. We develop patterns of thinking and speaking, and these patterns of thinking and speaking come from our past. Every experience we've ever had from the moment we took our first breath is created by us. Often, we get stuck in the muck and mire of misdirected conversations and thoughts. As you become more and more aware of and take responsibility for what you think and say, begin to notice your thoughts. Are they empowered or are they negative? Are they coming from some unfinished business from the past or are they coming from within? Re-member, you get to choose the thoughts and conversations you hold on to. The type of thoughts you hold on to determines what radiates from within. The character of the thought decides the actual nature of the experiences that will result from having that thought and speaking the words associated with it. We have been given the freedom of choice to select what we desire to think and speak. The power to choose our thoughts and our words becomes very powerful when we re-member the choice is ours. It is always up to us. We love to blame, and point fingers at others, our mother, father, or friends and co-workers. Every time we point a finger at others we forget that there are three fingers pointing right back at us.

We don't stop and think about the consequences of our words until it is often times too late. We don't think. Very often we react and respond, we don't stop and take a deep breath and think before we speak. Imagine the difference it would make if we thought before we spoke.

## Before you speak, THINK!

| T | *is it True?* |
| H | *is it Helpful?* |
| I | *is it Inspiring?* |
| N | *is it Necessary?* |
| K | *is it Kind?* |

~ Anon

Imagine what life would be like if we all took this anagram on as a matter of our word. We would have a new level of free time if we lived our lives like this.

## Food For Thought:

What is the impact of not thinking before you speak?

Can you see times where you did not think and created a mess?

What do you see possible for yourself if you thought before you spoke?

# You Are Either Expanding Or Contracting

The World Within is nothing short of a Universal Cornucopia of supply. The World Without is the drain to that supply. It's like pulling the stopper from the tub and watching the bath water go down the drain. Just how much abundance you receive depends on your willingness to recognize the Universal Cornucopia that is always waiting within you to deliver. You can receive as much as you believe you can. You have infinite energy and creative ability. Each of us is a channel, a passage and an opening to that limitless universal energy. Re-member, it takes a mental process and a commitment to produce a result. It really takes work. Mental action is the interaction you have upon the Universal Mind. The Universal Mind is the intelligence which covers all space and time and brings life to everything. This mental action and its reaction is the Law of Causation. We often think we cause things to happen, the small us in the world is our ego. We think big, we get big. We think small and we get just what we asked for every time, small. Just take a look at your life and what you have asked for, and look at what you have received.

The Law of Causation does not come from the individual; it comes from the Universal Mind. It is created by Source, The Divine, the All in All, The Creator or whatever you wish to call her. It is not objective, it is a subjective process. The results of this process show up in any number of ways.

Nothing can exist without the mind. If you are going to express life there must be mind. Everything which exists is some manifestation of the mind and will always be that. Remember you are constantly being bombarded by a whirlwind of mind energy, which I will call mind putty; likened to Silly Putty. This "mind putty" is alive and active. It takes the shape of that which the mind demands, or said another way...WHAT YOU THINK AND SAY. The thought provides the mold, the shape or matrix, which the substance of mind expresses. You create your words. Your words create your world. Remember, applying this thought process and understanding the Law of Causation will transform your life from without to within. Remember The Genius Lives Within.

| This is the natural order of the Laws of the Universe: | |
| --- | --- |
| THE WORLD WITHIN | THE WORLD WITHOUT |
| *Genius* | *Success* |
| *Abundance* | *All my needs are met* |
| *Harmony* | *Natural Flow* |
| *Creativity* | *Freedom* |
| *Love* | *Happiness* |
| *Joy* | *Satisfaction* |

| This is the world you are claiming… | This is the world you are creating… |
|---|---|
| THE WORLD WITHIN<br><br>*I'm not good enough*<br><br>*Unworthiness*<br><br>*Fear*<br><br>*Sickness*<br><br>*Depression* | THE WORLD WITHOUT<br><br>*Failure*<br><br>*Lack*<br><br>*Disease*<br><br>*Death*<br><br>*Suppression of ideas and life* |

## Question to Ponder:

What is the Source of all power?

# Thoughts Are Cause, And Conditions Are Effect

We must learn to control our thoughts so as to CREATE what we desire. Remember every thought is a cause, every condition its effect. All power is from within and under our control. When we begin to get this in the core of our being, we become conscious. A shift takes place in our consciousness in working together with this omnipotent law; it is the starting point of finding the Genius living within.

The majority of us live in the world of without. Only recently have a few of us found, and really accepted the truth of who we are, and endeavor to live from the world within. The World Within makes, creates, and essentially gives us the World Without. Our thoughts come from within first. Our thought creates our words and our words create our world. The World Within is creative and everything we find without has been created by our thoughts and words from our World Within.

| The World Within<br>CAUSE | The World Without<br>EFFECT |
|---|---|
| Change the CAUSE | Change the EFFECT |

This is not a new idea. It has been around for thousands and thousands of years. It is just a bit tough to wrap our thoughts around. Most of us make attempts to change the effect by working on the effect. Let's put it like this, I have no money, so I go to work on getting some money. All that I can see is I have no money. Said another way, we attempt to change the World Without by working on the World Without. This simply exchanges one form of distress for another. Notice, as hard as you try, things just never seem to change. To remove these dis-em-powered thoughts we must work on the cause. The cause can only be found in the World Within.

Here is a quote that crystallizes what I have been discussing:

> *"Cause and effect is as absolute*
> *and undeviating in the hidden*
> *realm of thought as in the world*
> *of visible and material things.*
> *Mind is the master weaver, both*
> *of the interior garment of*
> *character and the outer garment of*
> *circumstance."*
> *~James Allen*

Thought is creative energy and will naturally connect with its object and bring it into expression. It takes affirming and speaking into existence that which you desire. You must have faith. It takes silencing the "committee" in your head, those doubts and fears that keep you from honoring your Spirit! All that you hear in your head just before you fall asleep and as you awake in the morning is just noise. Many of us have grown up with the stories we created as a child and now we are a forty year old being driven and guided by a six year old. We forgot that we made decisions about the events of our life. When we were children things happened in our lives in the process of growing up. For instance you may have wet the bed, or your pet died or you saw mommy and daddy fussing with one another and you created a story about the event in order to survive it. You may feel you are not good enough, or that you are flawed or damaged goods as a result. Maybe you said, "I am unlovable" and then you believed it. You felt you were not good enough when you were seven and now you are forty seven, a college graduate, married, two teenage children, a husband/wife and the manager of 25 people at a major corporation. You manage a twenty two million dollar portfolio, a family and yet you still think you are not good enough. You walk around miserable and unfulfilled believing you are flawed, unlovable damaged goods.

*"Nothing can disturb you but your own thoughts. The suggestions, statements, or thoughts of other persons have no power. The power is within you and when your thoughts are focused on that which is good, then God's power is with your thoughts of good. There is only one creative power, and it moves as harmony. There are no divisions or quarrels in it. Its source is love. This is why God's power is with your thoughts of good."*

~ Dr. Joseph Murphy

## Questions to Think About:

Consider this statement: "I can't do it, I am not good enough, I am not worthy."

Is this the same statement you started saying to yourself when you were six years old?

If not what were you saying?

# All Is Energy

Are you worried about the future? No need to, the future is completely within your control. We are never at the mercy of some uncertain, external power unless we choose it. We have all been given free will and can agree that there is only one Source, one principle and unity of consciousness in the entire Universe. It is all powerful, all wise and ever present and it contains all thought and all things. It is within us all, and at all times, one consciousness which is omnipresent and present within everyone and everything. We are in it and also of it, so it follows that our consciousness is the same as this Universal Consciousness. All minds comprise the One Supreme Mind. The only difference is just how much you believe it.

## The Universal Mind

The Subconscious Mind connects us to the Universal Mind. The Universal Mind is the divinely infinite creative power of the entire universe and it is with us. The Universal Mind is always available and ready to assist us. We hold this energy in our bodies, in our chakras. Our Chakras are our body's main energy distribution system. They power up the magnetic sheath called the Aura, and the energy it produces surrounds us from the sole of our feet to about a foot above our heads. The Universal Mind and the Divine really do and can work together. They bring the objective idea and the subjective idea together perfectly. They work together, play together and cooperate, creating the fixed and the never-ending loop of our conciseness. All is energy. The Universal Mind is energy and it shows up through us. We are made from the same energy as the Universal Mind. So when we as individuals think a thought or speak a desire, it naturally links to its counterpart within the Universal Mind.

*"Mindfulness makes a full man. A full man speaks with an open mind. And like a parachute, the mind works better when it is fully opened. This awareness is the key to unlock the door from conflict and strife as well as wholesome thoughts emerge."*

~-Dr K Sri Dhammananda

## Question to Think About:

How are you related to the Universal Mind?

## Silent Contemplation

I would like you to consider the following Bible verse.

> *"I of myself can do nothing.*
> *It is the Spirit within who*
> *expresses and manifests as true*
> *success in my life." ~John 5:30*

Take in each word and its full meaning within the statement. Say it aloud and then read it silently to yourself. Pick out the word or words that have resonance or stand out for you. Do not write your responses, but thoughtfully consider them and simply note any reactions. As you ponder the words notice what thoughts arise? What are you beginning to become aware of? There is no right answer to the direction your thoughts will take. You might have the thought, "I don't get this" or "I understand this" or "What am I to do with this information?" It makes no differ-ence. Use this thought as you move into silent contemplation and see what thoughts come up. Stop all action and take a few moments to just think.

You will begin to realize that every time you have produced a successful result it came from within. It came from a place of unknown. You might have even said. "How did I do that?" You may have said, "Wow, what a surprise!" or "Where did that come from?" It came from within, it came from the Spirit within that you were born with, that is just waiting to express and bring forth your true success, accomplishments and your true passion.

When you were a child all your needs were met. All you had to do was begin to cry and you were given food, your diaper was changed or you were held and cuddled. You were kept safe in most cases and protected from all harm. You had the ability to get all you needed without having to do a thing so to speak.

You were a spiritual being beginning a human experience. As you grew more and more human, you lost touch with your spiritual connection as you were so busy becoming human. You left the World Within for the World Without. You stopped honoring your Spirit. You forgot the Genius Lives Within. All power comes from within. The answer to every question lives within us. We can hear it when we silently contemplate.

## Questions to Think About:

What had us forget that we were born spiritual beings?

What is it that has us remembering who we really are?

# Foundation Three

# Stillness Of The Mind

Now that you are beginning to become aware of your thoughts, and accepting the fact that your thoughts have been creating your words, and your words have been creating your world, I would like you to look at the reason you are reading this book. What are your thoughts and feelings about what you have read up to this point? What have you created that is working for you? What is not working in your life? Have you identified an area you desire to have a real breakthrough in? What are you beginning to be aware of about that area now? Remember, insight is revealed in the stillness of the mind. When faced with making a significant decision, you often search for a solution from a variety of sources. You may consider your past experiences; you may have conducted research, or asked a friend for an opinion. At the root of your search is a desire to receive trustworthy insight. The best source for receiving trustworthy insights and information is meditation. Learn to quiet your thoughts, silence your analytical mind, and go within. You will find the answers in the silence. It takes a willingness to be still and go within. As you practice meditating by sitting in stillness, you begin to quiet the constant chatter that is always present. This presents you with the opportunity to hear that still small voice that has been waiting for you to tune in. It takes practice being self-disciplined and operating with a high level of integrity. This is a practice and a habit, a practice and habit worth having.

When you rest in the silence it may not look as if anything is happening and, you are tapping into a rich vein of spiritual resources. You are gaining loads of strength to maneuver around any and every obstacle that may arise. You will begin to realize you have all that you need to move through the tight spaces in your life that show up in the World Without.

The two main reasons for human suffering are anxiety and dis-ease and they can be easily traced to not following some of the natural laws. This is owing to the fact that so far, knowledge about the natural laws has remained largely unknown. The gray clouds of doom and gloom which have accumulated over time are beginning to roll away, and with them, many of the upsets and breakdowns that go along with not honoring your Spirit. The outside world leaves us struggling to operate with integrity and prevents us from honoring our self as our word, and keeping our promises and agreements. The inner world is given by 100% integrity, workability and wholeness; the results we are looking for and so much more.

*Guidance is revealed in the stillness of my mind*
~ Unity

## Question to Ponder:

What does it takes to truly discover the Genius that lives within?

# You Get To Choose

One of the wonderful things about us is that we are given the freedom of choice. Yes, we have free will. We can do whatever we want to do, the good, the bad and the ugly. We are free to decide how we respond to life. We get to choose how we react. When a barrier blocks a stream, the water finds a way to flow over, under or around it. Sometimes the stream gathers strength and moves with force and speed through narrow passages, other times it collects and rests in shallow pools. We are free to choose the course of our life's direction and to determine the flow of our life. You are free to choose the course of your life's direction and you get to determine the natural flow of your life force. You get to say how your life goes. You always have and you always will. Look at what life has given you. You created it. I know it might be a hard pill to swallow and you may even refuse to go for it. You chose the path you wished to take. You choose to get an education or not. You choose to live wherever you live. You choose to work where you work. You even choose to eat what you eat or drink what you drink. You choose to be a victim or a victor. You choose to live or to die. You choose to laugh or cry. You choose to sow the life seeds you sowed. You choose to keep your word or not. You had all these thoughts and you held them as your truth.

When a thought is held as truth, the Universal Subconscious Mind takes action on it. It makes no distinction between good or bad, right or wrong, positive or negative; thinking makes it so. If you say you cannot do something, then you cannot do it. If you say you are broke, then you are broke. When you say you are not worthy or good enough, then you become not worthy or not good enough. You say, I hate, and then you hate. You say, I am wrong, and then you are wrong. Your words are always creating your reality but you must remember that you get to choose what you say. You get to create your world.

You have to train yourself to keep your security guard on duty 24/7, 365. Your security guard is your protection against anything that keeps you from honoring your Spirit. What happens during times of anger, panic, nervousness and stress? How do these emotions show up for you when or if the security guard is away or on break? When you are in the presence of others you could be subject to influences that make you feel victimized or under attack. You can become open to the consequences of increased anger, panic and stress and may lead to other self-deprecating thoughts and actions, all based on fear that has been allowed to run rampant. You hold on to these thoughts as if they are the truth but they are not the truth. You make them your truth, whether they are good or bad, true or false or right or wrong. These dis-empowered ideas then hang around and create a downward spiral of energy that diminishes your life force. You must constantly and consistently guard your Subconscious Mind from unhealthy and negative thoughts. The effects of not doing so can last a very long time, often creating a lifetime of unnecessary misery and suffering.

The Subconscious Mind picks up through intuition and moves very fast, and it never sleeps or takes a rest. Just as your heart continually beats and breathing is automatic, your Subconscious Mind is always working. The Bible says, "Anything you ask for in my name you shall receive." Take a look at your life and notice when you have received the gifts you have asked for. When and where have you asked, and received that which you have said you desire? You have undoubtedly done it successfully many, many times. Your Subconscious Mind is connected to the Universal Mind, the Omnipotent. If you ask your subconscious mind with vehement passion for a certain result to be produced and you have absolute faith and belief in it, it shall be so. This is a law, just like the Law of Gravity and you want to master it. Remember your Subconscious Mind is the seat of your soul. It is the root of your ideals and dreams. It is the soil in which your creative seeds are sown, nurtured and then sprout.

The Subconscious Mind cannot defend itself, so if it is given negative impute it takes some strong counter information to remove it. How many years have you been feeding your subconscious mind negative input? It takes practice to keep the negative input at bay. You must practice not allowing negative thoughts and ideas to infiltrate your Subconscious Mind, it is do-able! I'm not saying it's going to be easy or it will happen overnight. Choosing to make clear choices means you get to say how your life goes. It takes practice and practice again, until it becomes habitual and routine. The mind must accept this practice as the answer to keeping the negative away. Take a look at two successful athletes, Venus and Serena Williams. They have been practicing for a very long time. When they were little girls, their dad had them out at the local neighborhood tennis courts hitting tennis balls. They played all the time, and it became a habit to them. Practice has to become a new habit for you, and a habit that is worth having. Look at their success. Today they are world class tennis professionals with many awards, prizes, trophies, honors and much money. They are at the top of their game and they operate with a very high level of integrity and discipline. In other words they honor their Spirit.

Be gentle with yourself as you create and invent new habits. More often than not we are very hard on ourselves when we say we have messed up or failed. It goes back to our childhood when we were punished, beaten or chastised for not succeeding or messing up. Our parents could only do the very best they knew how. They were taught by their parents who did the best they could. Now, look at how far we have come in understanding who we really are. We are descendants of the Ultimate Source, so be gentle with yourself as you take on creating habits worth having.

The Universal Mind within is always ready and able to assist us. Many coaches have said, to begin to have anything become habitual you must do it for at least 21 days in a row. Do it at about the same time and in the same way, each day and it will become a habit. Therefore, start off creating a habit of being aware of what you are thinking. This will evolve into a new way of life; a way of life that produces the lasting effects and results you desire. New behaviors become ingrained into your Universal Subconscious Mind and then the results become automatic.

Write down what you are thinking. Create a thought journal and capture your first thoughts upon waking in the morning or after a meditation. It is best if the new habit is simple, nothing too complicated or rough. Have compassion for yourself and take it easy. If the new habit is too difficult or stressful it will only reinforce harmful or negative thought patterns. If you take this practice on, your always patient, forever listening, Subconscious Mind will take on the new habit and produce the desired results.

> *"Don't talk about the way you are.*
> *Talk about the way you want to be."*
> ~Anonymous

On the physical side, the subconscious rules your vital life processes, enabling you to restore health and balance to your body. On the mental side, the subconscious holds your memory, and it is the foundation of all your habits. On the spiritual side, the subconscious is the root of your inspirations and aspirations and ignites your imagination. It is the pathway to recognizing Universal Source. To the degree that you realize this Divine energy is yours, is the degree to which you come into a greater understanding of the source of all power and the Genius that Lives Within. The entire Universal Mind is creative, and creativity is the only action the mind possesses, therefore thoughts that flow from it must then be creative. There is a big difference between just having thoughts and directing your thoughts constructively, systematically and with conscious effort. As you with practice, guide your thought, it will come into harmony with the Universal Mind. You are in tune with the Infinite and you direct the operation of the mightiest force in existence. In fact, you are in tune with the Infinite Universal Mind and all your needs are met. It is called being present to the Genius that Lives Within. This creative force will line up with your directed thoughts and bring them into fruition as you honor your Spirit.

## Food for Thought:

What is the importance of guarding your Subconscious Mind?

# Begin To Think Differently

At this present moment, I believe the Universal mind wants us to know that, we are what we think of all day long. Day after day, week after week, month after month our thoughts shape us just as dripping water shapes a rock. It says to us, "Pay attention" to what you are consistently thinking about. Are your thoughts serving you? A gentle reminder about practices, re-member to jot down your thoughts and be aware of what you are thinking at all times. Meditate and practice stilling the body as you prepare to still the chatter in your mind. I like to call that chatter our "Committee," those ever present voices that claim our attention. The "Committee" is the last thing you hear before you fall asleep and the first thing you hear when you wake up in the morning. The more often you can "Be still and know that you are God," the deeper into stillness you will go.

## Recognizing Genius Lives Within

The ability to receive and manifest our power depends on our ability to recognize Divine energy or Genius living within us. This energy is constantly creating and re-creating and is prepared at any moment to produce results through our thoughts. Whatever we think, it will produce. Whether it is good, bad or ugly is up to us. The way the mind within works is that it utilizes two matching modes of movement, or parallel energies. One is conscious and the other subconscious. And if we think we can see the complete range of mind action simply by looking through our own consciousness, then we are missing the mark. That is like attempting to light all of New York City with a pen-light. The subconscious, allows us to move forward with promise and determination. This would be impossible if there was the slightest possibility of a mistake in the Universal Mind. We haven't any idea of how it works or what makes it happen. It works to create the perfect conditions and supplies all that is needed for our overall benefit. It essentially drops perfectly ripened fruit into our laps with no effort from us required. Then, the final analysis of our thought process shows that our subconscious is the stage of the most essential mental phenomena of our time on this energy plane. To know that everything in existence is ours for the asking is one of the greatest truths yet to be realized.

## Question to Ponder:

What are the actions of The Universal Mind?

# Let Go And Let Life Happen

Ease and perfection show up in our lives the minute we allow it to. The amount we surrender to our Subconscious Mind as we stop depending on the Conscious Mind is the perfect course of action. Coming from the Subconscious Mind, which is always perfectly aligned for our highest good, we can achieve our wildest dreams. What is the main importance of your subconscious? It inspires you; allows you to access information when you need it and warns you when you are in danger. Inspiration sometimes takes the form of memories, dreams, and images that the Subconscious Mind has saved and makes available to you through your memories and awareness.

This same subconscious guides how you think, gives you your unique sense of style and individual flair. It is capable of accomplishing things that are too complicated for the Conscious Mind to even imagine.

When you become aware of how much you depend on your subconscious, you become aware of new possibilities. You start to see yourself thriving, achieving and accomplishing things. You'll wonder to yourself "How did I do that?" When you let go and let life happen it will; and it will do so miraculously. Regarding the Conscious Mind, you cannot stop the beating of your heart or the digestion of food to nourish your body or the elimination of waste or any other vital life process that are occurring all the time. The human mind receives more than 220,000 thoughts every day. Some of them you will choose to act upon and others you will let passively float by. As you re-member, thoughts and more thoughts come through you like waves on the beach; in and out, breaking and returning back out to sea.

When you look at these two types of energy, conscious and subconscious energy, you can see that one is given by the present and the other is given by the invisible movement and magic of the Universal Mind. We seem to be blown away by the one mind while taking the other for granted. The two energy fields are powers of the Conscious or Objective Mind which relates to the World Within and the Subconscious or the Subjective Mind which allows and makes physical life possible. The conscious mind has the ability to discriminate and is given the power of choice. Some of us have learned to use the Conscious Mind at a very high level. Have you ever been told you are "strong willed?" If so then you also have the ability to impress other minds and even guide and direct the Subconscious Mind of others. People who can do this are often times called charismatic. The Conscious Mind can overtake the Subconscious Mind which can have a dramatic effect and alter the direction of your life. The choices you make in life are a demonstration of this. Notice, when fear, lack, disease and imbalance show up. When this happens you have allowed dis-empowered and false suggestions to be accepted as truth by a vulnerable subconscious mind. An empowered mind or a mind that has practiced and practiced guarding the subconscious mind can prevent the invasion of dis- empowered thoughts. You can place your own "security guard" at the door of your subconscious. It takes your will and the fulfillment of the wishes of the Universal Mind to keep the dis-empowered and false suggestions out. It takes self discipline.

> *"The great law of substitution is the answer to fear. Whatever you fear has its solution in the form of your desire. If you are sick, you desire health. If you are in the prison of fear, you desire freedom. Expect the good. Mentally concentrate on the good, and know that your Subconscious Mind answers you always. It never fails."*

~Dr. Joseph Murphy

The Conscious Mind is where you will from, it is automatic and instinctive. Every action you have seen, heard and experienced informs you in a very important way. Your Subconscious Mind pulls from the information given to you from the world without. When the information is true, accurate, and empowered you come to perfect and powerful solutions and answers based on information given to the Subconscious Mind. When the suggestions are incorrect, untrue or dis-empowered, the Subconscious Mind does not consider that these suggestions are negative. It relies on your security guard to keep unconstructive and pessimistic information from getting in. The Subconscious Mind says, if the security guard has let it in, then it must be okay.

## Question to Ponder:

What is the importance of managing your thoughts?

# Meditation

What is meditation? It is a pathway to attaining balance, inner peace and calmness. Meditation is the practice of being in the silence; being still and listening. Sitting and listening for that still, small voice to arise from within. Meditation differs from prayer in that it is primarily an opportunity to silence the "committee" of the mind and bring about insights and remembering that has become present day knowledge. Meditation is not an abstract activity as it is frequently considered to be. It takes concentration, release, surrender, clear concentration on your breathing and being still so that the Universal Subconscious mind and speak to you, giving you ideas and thoughts. As we meditate we can create and experience our thoughts on our mental screen. With each meditation practice and I do call it a practice a spiritual practice we gain greater ability to visualize the ways and means of bringing them into manifestation. While prayer will always be a foundational approach for many of us, the present-day development of intellect demands a more mental form of inner action: meditation is of a creative nature and having a positive and scientific method of working with the Laws

Where does it begin? It all starts with breathing. To get yourself settled and grounded breathe, breathe, and breathe again. Take three rich, deep breaths to begin. Each breath goes deeper and deeper within. Breath and breathing are the very first gifts given to us from the Divine. When we were carried in our mother's womb we swam in fluid. Then, when we died from mother's womb and were born into this energy plane, we took our first earthly breath. Some of us gagged, coughed and cried. Many of us never took that first breath. They are called "Still born." Some of us smiled and cooed as we took our first breath. Now years later we are still here and continue to breathe 24/7, taking our breath for granted.

We have forgotten that our very first breath on this earthly plane was a gift. It is a gift that has the power to bring you back to the present moment the second you become aware of it. What I mean by the present moment is the NOW, not the past of yesterday, several hours ago or even a few seconds ago. By taking a deep breath you are in the present moment.

The future has not occurred yet. You are only here now. As you watch yourself breathe in deeply visualize the air filling your lungs. Notice your solar plexus is rising and falling with each breath.

While sitting privately in a quiet, comfortable, and peaceful location, let your thoughts roam. Begin to settle down by taking several deep breaths. Your thoughts will calm down in time. Start with sitting for at least 5 to 10 minutes. Allow yourself to work up to 20 minutes or longer. With practice and patience you can easily extend your meditation time. If you become distracted just say to yourself, Noise. Then take several deep breathes and place your attention on your breathing. Practice this at least 3 times a day, every day. Do this 24/7, 365 days a year; yes EVERYDAY! The more you practice, the easier it will become and the better you will become at meditating. Re-read through this meditation process again and then stop reading and begin a meditation.

Take five or ten minutes to practice what you have just read before reading on.

Some of you will find this very difficult, others will have no problem. Either way is okay really. Allow yourself permission to be exactly where you are and to be gentle with yourself. Meditate at least three times a day, do it until you can do it with ease. Practice meditating until it becomes a part of you. Your day will not feel complete unless you have practiced your meditation. You'll find yourself looking forward to doing it. Meditation is essential to the process of realizing the Genius Lives Within.

During the time you practice meditation, become aware, look at yourself and begin to see just how much your thoughts have created your life. If you say to yourself, *"That's jacked up, or what's wrong with me, why did I do that?"* Stop and allow yourself to be aware of what you are saying. You are assessing yourself. You are judging yourself. You may even be putting yourself down or lifting yourself up, it doesn't matter. Just notice without judgment or opinions, as you become aware that you are just talking, yes, talking to yourself! Take responsibility for your talking and let your thoughts go. Release what you have been saying to yourself to the Universe. Let it go.

Know that it is always your choice. You have free will to do as you please. Practice being aware of your thoughts, the ones you choose to hold on to, and the one you choose to let go of so as to create an open vessel to be filled by the Genius That Lives Within. The benefits of meditation are numerous. Here are just a few for you to think about.

- *Relaxes the nervous system*

- *Lowers Blood pressure*

- *Releases fears*

- *Reduces anxiety*

- *Relieves depression*

- *Frees us from self-doubt and quiets our internal chatter, "The Committee"*

- *Restores balance to our digestive system and supports digestion*

- *Diminishes the intensity of headaches/migraines*

- *Creates optimism, confidence and self-motivation*

- *Releases creativity*

# Several Additional Reasons To Meditate

You will begin to experience your feelings. Everything that you have been attempting to hold back or hide profound sadness, guilt, shame, anger and fear will show up during meditation. Let them when these feelings can be seen in the light of meditation they will disappear. You will stop lying to yourself. When you lie to yourself you are really lost. As you experience your true feelings the ability to fool yourself will become more and more difficult. You will begin to take full responsibility for yourself and your thoughts.

You will stop fooling others. When you stop lying to yourself it becomes extremely difficult to lie to others. Your light will begin to shine and the truth will set you free. You might have to forgive and tell others how much you truly care about them. Or that you need assistance of some sort. Meditation is a humbling experience.

As you take on meditation as a practice you will realize you are not all that busy. Everyone is just so "Busy" these days. Doing this that or the other is the excuse we use. We do not stop and take time for ourselves. Meditation is for you and only you. It causes you to stop and take a "timeout" for yourself.

# Foundation Four

# Sowing Seeds Of Faith

Faith comes to us when we cease to think of external things having power over us and realize that Source-- which is all powerful--brings good into manifestation through us. We increase our faith in God as we realize that in reality there is only one: The Divine. No other power exists. When you wake up in the morning anticipate seeing the good and glorious activity of Spirit in the day that lay ahead of you. Have faith that the goodness of your Higher Power is now being made manifest in, through and around you. Look for miracles to appear everywhere. That is all. Approaching every situation from the standpoint of absolute faith in Source, and you'll find worries and doubts are short-lived. Faith brings answers to prayer, and visible and tangible evidence of the goodness of the Most High. Have absolute faith in the goodness of The Divine manifesting in your life right now and it will.

Plant into your subconscious, seeds of unwavering belief with faith and you will reap the full harvest of that which you believe.

> *Whatever you ask for in prayer, believe that you*
> *have received it, and it will be yours.*
> ~Mark 11:24

## Question to Ponder:

What does faith give you?

# Affirmations

Affirmations are a practice that will allow all that we dream, imagine and desire to emerge; to come from within us. Remember, we were born perfect. We have everything we need right where we are. Affirmations are always positive. Affirmations are short and sweet and not something you necessarily reclaim from the past, you create them newly. What you create becomes your affirmation so affirm your desires with faith; believing you have already received that which you affirm. Let them arise from the silence of your meditations. Here are a few examples of affirmations you can use as you begin the process:

**Affirmations**:

**Accomplishment** - *I call on the Divine within who bestows upon me joy, peace and success.*

**Beginnings** - *With ease and grace the birth of the perfect is possible.*

**Calm** - *The love of the Divine holds me in the palm of her hand, safety and protection surround me I can relax.*

**Confidence -** *I can express myself with ease and I have no fear.*

**Divine Order** - *Everything is perfect. Divine Intelligence flows through me. I let go and let God.*

**Faith -** *I believe in the omnipotence of God. The one and only God is present in me.*

**Guidance** - *Peace be still. I listen for your wisdom, I speak your words and I feel your direction.*

**Happiness -** *I claim my joy now. No one or nothing can take away my happiness. I am in the presence of the glory of God. I am getting better and better every day.*

**Health** - *Physician heal thyself…The temple of the living God is within, your will for me is perfect health.*

**Joy** - *No one or nothing can steal my joy. Joy pours forth from me as a wellspring, I am free and happy.*

**Prosperity** - *Abundance is mine; I am rich with the love of God. All my needs are met.*

**Relations -** *I give 100% of myself to receive 100% of others. I am love, loved and loving.*

**Success** - *Success is mine. Spirit leads the way and I am victorious.*

**Thanksgiving** - *I stand in the presence of gratitude. I am grateful for each new moment of each new day.*

**Wholeness** - *Everything is perfect, the Divine is perfect. We are all perfect in the eyes of the Divine..*

You can write your own personal affirmations.

# Chakras: The Body's Energy Center

Our bodies are an amazing example of Divine Intelligence. They are the vehicle through which we maneuver in the physical world. Into them we breathe life and have our being. They are the machine through which we power our lives. And within our miraculous bodies are contained Chakras or energy centers that allow us to meet the physical, mental and emotional demands of daily life. These energy centers connect us to the world within and manifest the world without. When fully functioning, they are a direct connection to Source, allowing a free flowing channel of Divine guidance and inspiration. When blocked we are cut off from the Universal Mind and fail to embrace the full potential of what otherwise flows through us naturally. Remember we are energy, connected to everything around us and when our energy channels are blocked, Universal energy cannot flow through us. We become essentially separated from that which we are. Below is a short description of each of the Chakras and how they function. Take a moment to read each, give yourself permission to connect to the Divine energy and guidance they provide.

## The Chakra System

Chakras play a part in helping you connect with higher guidance and your natural intuitive sense. In order to make better decisions, have a clearer sense of direction and enjoy deeper peace of mind it is important to understand how the Chakra System works. The Chakra System begins at the base of the spine and work upwards. They ascend along the spinal column and number from one to seven. The first or Root Chakra is located at the base of the spine. The second or Sacral Chakra is located in the lower abdomen area. The third or Solar Plexus is located in the belly area. The fourth or Heart Chakra is located in the center of the chest. The fifth or Throat Chakra is located at the base of the throat. The sixth or third Eye Chakra is located in the center of the forehead and the seventh or Crown Chakra is located at the top of the head.

These energy centers are crucial to integrating the energy and information you receive from your higher self and the Divine. If the Chakras are weak or closed, you may experience symptoms. This can include disease, a sense of aimlessness and feeling spiritually empty. All of which can lead to making wrong choices and decisions in your career and personal life. You may even experience difficulty with finding and connecting to your life's purpose. When your Chakras are open and fully functioning, you will achieve balance and inner harmony in living your life and expressing all that is within you.

These techniques will help you open and strengthen your Chakras. I strongly urge you to try them. You will notice a definite difference in your energy level. The more you practice the more vibrant and alive you will feel. You will feel a greater sense of aliveness and find yourself more focused and centered.

**CROWN CHAKRA** (above the top of your head)

The Crown Chakra is the seventh Chakra. It is your direct connection to Source and your Higher Self. Its energy flows out of your body and receives energy at the same time. The Crown Chakra is the fuel behind the Divine inspiration we receive. The energy of the Crown Chakra influences your experience with charity, connection to a higher power, divinity, belief systems, revelations and Divine consciousness. The therapeutic gemstone that feeds the Crown Chakra is clear quartz, and its color is violet or purple. Try wearing something purple and let it lift your spiritual vibration.

Practice this to open the Crown Chakra

Write the following statements in your journal, IPad, cell phone or mirror.

- I am vital to divine consciousness
- I am joined to my highest self
- I am linked to the higher purpose of money
- I am following my divine path

- I am living my purpose

- I am spiritually connected to the Divine.

Next, place your hands on the top of your head and gently pull them apart as if revealing a secret opening at the top of your head. Do this while repeating each of the statements above. Remember to breathe as you repeat the words and feel your energy level rising. Wear something purple or violet every day for a whole week! You'll be amazed at the amount of energy you have. When your Crown Chakra is open and fully functioning, you'll find yourself getting things done with time and energy to spare.

## THIRD EYE OR INTUITIVE CHAKRA (the center of your forehead)

Your sixth chakra or Third Eye Chakra is your psychic power - your intuitive knowing - and is often referred to as your third eye. It is responsible for your experience with intuition and psychic talents, self-reflection, visualization, imagination, perception, discernment, and how to develop clarity and trust your intuition. The color for the sixth Chakra is indigo. The therapeutic gemstone or crystal for this chakra is amethyst. It is one of my favorite gemstones, and I have used it extensively over the years to help strengthen my intuition and discernment. Wear something purple or carry an amethyst to give your third eye a big boost and get in touch with your own inner psychic powers.

Try this to open a blocked Third Eye Chakra. For a whole week, write the following statements in your journal or commit them to memory.

- I am discerning

- I am motivated

- I am receiving guidance for my life

- I am discriminating

- I am aware of my higher purpose

- I am honoring my Spirit

- I have a balanced and powerful sixth Chakra

Next, put your little finger on the middle of your forehead, and imagine you are opening a closed eye while stating each of the above affirmations. Do this daily for the entire week and see life open up right before your eyes. Our intuition is one of the tools we have available to help direct us through life. By unblocking your third eye, you are bringing forth your greatest resource for Divine direction - so trust your intuition and your spiritual eyes to guide you.

## THROAT CHAKRA (At the base of the throat)

Your fifth chakra is your Throat Chakra it is the location of your voice. You speak the power of this Chakra. Everything you claim about yourself and your world comes from the words you speak. You literally speak your existence utilizing this Chakra. The therapeutic gemstones or crystal associated with this Chakra is Lapis its color is blue with little flakes of gold. Symptoms of a weak or closed Throat Chakra include feeling unheard. You feel like nobody cares about your opinions or what you have to say. You feel silenced or suppressed and stifled. When your Throat Chakra is closed or blocked you may suffer from sore throats and respiratory problems. Remember…there is no other voice like yours, and no other Spirit like yours. Let it be heard and honored.

Try this exercise to open and heal the Throat Chakra. For an entire week write in your journal the following statements: Then meditate on these words.

- I speak my truth

- I am clear and kind

- I am uplifted by my truth

- I am my own power

- I am hearing my still small voice

- I express myself without difficulty

- I am here to share my uniqueness.

Every morning repeat the above statements while rubbing on your throat or collarbone with two fingers. This will to help open up this energy center and release the power of your voice.

**HEART CHAKRA** (the center of your chest)The fourth Chakra is the Heart Chakra and it bridges the higher and lower Chakras. When you Heart Chakra is open and strong, you'll experience, loving and emphatic relationships with your loved ones, your co-workers and people in your life. You will feel a heartfelt sense of gratitude and appreciate how perfect and wonderful your life really is. The color that represents the Heart Chakra is green and the therapeutic gemstone or crystal for this Chakra is Rose quartz. Nature is abounding with this color. Green helps us heal and creates a strong life force for all living things. It gives a sense of aliveness and rejuvenation when you feel rundown. For a quick me up put on something green and feel your energy grow. Drink a glass of freshly made green juice in the morning and feel your body energize and come alive.

Try this for opening the Heart Chakra. Practice this affirmation on your Heart Chakra for at least a week. Write the following statements in your journal and on your screen saver, and every morning during the week as you recite these words, place your right hand on your Heart Chakra, and breathe in the thought of the color green. It will leave you refreshed, rejuvenated and ready for action. Hold the Rose quartz gem stone for the Heart Chakra in your hand or place it on your chest or a nearby shelf or table.

- I am loved from the moment I was born

- I am secure in feeling my feelings

- I am a balanced and energetic Heart Chakra

- I am protected to give and receive love

- I am loving myself and giving out that love

- I forgive, I forgive, I forgive

- I am supported by the Divine.

Do this every day for seven days and your heart will be content. You will be happier more alive and loving.

## SOLAR PLEXIS CHAKRA (In your upper abdomen just above the navel)

The third Chakra, the Solar Plexus or Personal Power Chakra is your power center. Your Personal Power Chakra is all about your power and identity. When you were a child around the age of 5, your developmental need was to know you had power, and that you could use that power to define your unique self and make your mark in the world. The therapeutic gemstone associated with this Chakra is citrine. The color for the Solar Plexus Chakra is yellow. Like the sun, think of this energy center as an ener-gizer. It is the body's spiritual energy center and it can give you the energy and guidance to power your life in the direction you seek. If your parents did not validate or empower you as a child, then your Personal Power Chakra may have slowed down or be under-developed. The great thing about this Chakra is that it is never too late to get it charged up to full power. Symptoms of a weak or closed Solar Plexus Chakra include struggling with self-esteem issues, and feelings of unworthiness. You may feel powerless to change your circumstances or see options for yourself. You may also suffer from frequent stomach aches, gas or have bowel problems which can cause anxiety and stress.

Try this for opening the Solar Plexus Chakra. Work on your Solar Plexus for an entire week. Write the following statement in your journal and on your bathroom mirror and repeat it several times.

*I am powerful, and I am using my power to better my life and my world for the benefit of all mankind. I am getting better and better every day.*

This is a very powerful statement! Every morning place your hands on your lower abdomen and feel the energy. Starting your day affirming your power will increase the amount that is available to you throughout the rest of your day. You can also do this simple exercise any time during the day for an instant energy boost.

## SACRAL CHAKRA (in your pelvic area.)

The second Chakra is the Sacral or Sexual Chakra. This Chakra has a direct influence on your sexuality, and has everything to do with creativity. When it is strong you are able to have positive sexual experiences and view sexuality in a positive light. The health of this Chakra is responsible for keeping you passionate about your partner and your life in general. The therapeutic gemstone associated with this

Chakra is carnelian. The color is orange. Wear orange clothing to nourish the Sacral Chakra and wake up this powerful and wonderfully creative power source.

Try this exercise for strengthening and energizing your Sacral Chakra:

For a week, put the statements listed below on your mirror and in your personal journal. Repeat them while rotating your fist on you pelvis in a clockwise direction, envision turning a wheel and feel the power generated from the rotation of your hands. As you do this you will make safe the truths you are repeating and feel the power within you become available.

- Thank You, Mother/Father God.

- I give love and am worthy of love

- I am grateful to be born

- My life is perfect

- I deserve of all of life's pleasures

- I am grateful for my body as it is now

- I am comfortable in my skin

- I am welcoming, nurturing and comfortable

- I welcome contribution.

Healing your ROOT CHAKRA (at the base of your spine)

Your primary Chakra or Root Chakra holds the energy force that influences all of our birth issues, life existence, routines, inherited family patterns, finances, health issues, connectedness, and safety.

The therapeutic gemstone of this Chakra is Ruby and its color is red. The color red is a very strong color and can be over-whelming for some people especially if this Chakra is blocked. Try wearing something red this week, a scarf or some other accessories a ring or earrings, socks or dare to assert yourself to whatever degree you are comfortable with.

This will support the healing of your Root Chakra.

Place your right fist on your Root Chakra, which is your groin area. Pull your fist forward as if removing a stopper from the tub. Make a sideways figure eight movement bringing your fist to your heart area and back again. Make this motion several times as you repeat the following words.

- I belong because I am alive

- It is my birthright to be wealthy and abundant

- I release all negative energy related to my birth

- I release past baggage and beliefs that hold me down

- I am rooted and connected as I share all my gifts

- I am balanced and at peace in my first Chakra.

Do this daily for at least a week and you will shift the energy of your Root Chakra so that it is in perfect alignment and raises its vibrational frequency. A strong and powerful Root Chakra provides a foundation for getting the result you desire and supports your ability to hold on to them. As you work with your Root Chakra expect to see a shift in your life circumstances.

## And while you are at it...

Give a boost to your abundance power in your bodies account. Begin by closing your eyes and imagining a bucket pouring gold coins down into your body's bank account. See it; hear it, filling your account. Whatever amount comes to mind, imagine that it is already there and much more is on the way. Remember you can have as much as you are able to imagine.

# What Are You Resisting?

What are you holding on to that is not working? What are you unwilling to surrender? What are you resisting? The surrendering of whatever it is you are holding on to would make all the difference. Allow yourself to let go into the silence. Release anything you might be holding on to. Notice what you are still holding onto that is no longer working. Be with what you are holding onto without judgment or opinions and then release it. Some of us are afraid of showing up great in our own lives. What can happen if you gave up your fear of being great, of being fabulous of showing up one hundred percent and letting your light shine? You will become great and fabulous without fear while being courageous. There would be nothing in between us and our greatness. When we can give up the thought and fear of being wrong or bad and stop judging ourselves, then we can be who we really are, which is magnificent. When you consciously accept that there is nothing to fear, that your light is shining and you are one with the Universal Mind, you will have come into ownership of your natural God given birthright. When you really understand that you are energy and energy cannot be created or destroyed, then you will have begun to acknowledge that a Genius Lives Within.

The more you release fear, the freer you become to hear the voice of your Universal Mind. Allow the voice of your Universal Guide the opportunity to speak to you. If you are walking in the wrong direction you can stop, turn around, and go in a different direction as you please. Be courageous. You have fear and you are not stopped by your fear.

You can also change the direction of your thinking if you wish. If you are having stressful, upsetting or annoying thoughts and you want to feel empowered, just change your thoughts. Think about what gives you joy, what stimulates your creativity and what lights you up about being alive. Start by thinking about the things that make you happy, uplifted and satisfied. Think about what a positive difference you make as you help others or take good care of yourself. You are in action when you do this; begin to feel and experience a zest for life. All it takes is a shift in your thinking to make the difference.

Take on loving yourself and all of your greatness and stop resisting. Love yourself as you are. No one is any more or less unique than you are. There are millions of blades of grass and billions of individuals on the planet and we are all different. Re-member the Universal mind is the source from which everything comes. It is one with our Subconscious Mind, which has created everything.

## FEAR

What is the biggest impediment to accessing the World Within? Fear; is the enemy of the Universal mind. Fear is something you hold onto consciously and unconsciously. Often, it doesn't show up like fear or panic, instead it shows up in your thoughts and in your words. When you say things like oh, I'm not good enough or you can't make me do that, or why I should, or any number of negative statements you tell yourself, this is fear. Fear prevents you from taking action and keeps you stuck in a pattern of inaction which keeps you from the things you desire. When we have no fear, we have full confidence in everything that is good and true. Franklin D. Roosevelt famously said, "The only thing to really fear is fear itself." If you are experiencing a lack of confidence notice that fear is very nearby. When you begin to realize the Genius Lives Within and that there is nothing to fear, then you are beginning to develop inner spiritual strength and vision. You start to understand that good is everlasting and everything else is temporary. Fear is not a thing you can put your hands around, it is an all pervasive thought that fools you into inaction. It is a thought that you believe in until you make it real in your mind. As you control our thoughts you can control your fear. Realize that fear is a liar, it is not real. More often than not you are afraid of a conversation, or words or some future outcome that has yet to appear. Fear does not come from the World Within; fear comes from the World Without. Take on, going within using meditation, prayer, affirmation and honoring your Spirit as a practice. This practice will support you in putting fear in it proper place. Putting fear aside will allow for the presence of love to begin to show up everywhere.

Take for instance the game of baseball. In baseball, the batter has to bat ten times just to make three out of ten bats. Think about players who made it into The Hall of Fame, how many bats do you think they had to make? They had to make three out of ten bats. The average batter makes two or 2 ½ bats out of ten. Now think about how many players there are and how few actually make it to the Hall of Fame. The ones that take action and make the most of each bat are those that make it into the Hall of Fame. Your ability to direct and change your thinking is your opportunity to take action on the inspiration and guidance from your Universal Mind. What you think is what gets produced in the objective world NOW. Notice how it always happens this way. It is a law, a Universal Law.

> *"The only jinx that follows anyone is a fear thought repeated over and over in the mind. Break the jinx by knowing that whatever you start you will bring to a conclusion in divine order. Picture the happy ending and sustain it with confidence."*
>
> -Dr Joseph Murphy

When life gets hectic, you may feel pressured to move quickly, however you have another option. Stop and take three deep breaths. It only takes a few seconds, yet it makes a world of difference. Breathe in and out, fully and deeply. Mindfully take a breath in and slowly, mindfully release it. Notice that you are centered, focused and at peace. Calm washes over you. These few moments give the mind, body and spirit a mini-break. Meditation is a must to quiet your mind. When you quiet your mind you can hear the still small voice, direct and inspire you. You must practice. When you stop practicing you lose the ability to quickly access that place of stillness that is your birthright. When you are able to come from that place of stillness you make only the appropriate choices and you are clear and present. You will achieve the desired results. Remember you have all you need to meet any challenge. With your mind now quiet and calm, you can return to your day open and receptive. Perhaps you've even had an *Aha* moment or two! Be thankful as you remember to take a few moments throughout the day to practice your breathing. The results you will begin to achieve will inspire you to continue.

Remember, all that you desire is waiting for you.

*"You will find him if you search after him with all your heart and soul."*
~Deuteronomy 4:29

You must become the witness of your life with no judgment, story or opinions. You possess all the power when you take responsibility for your actions. Being responsible will allow you to take the steps you need to take right now to fulfill on that which you really want in your life. Look to see if there are any "clean-up" conversations that need to be had with yourself and or others. What I mean by clean up conversations is, addressing anyone including yourself that you have made wrong, judged, invalidated or tried to control. If these circumstances exist then there are "clean up conversations" for you to have. Set a time to have them if you must. By having these conversations, you are no longer resisting what must be done; you are acting with a high level of integrity, self-discipline and honoring your Spirit.

*"Excess drinking and drugging is an unconscious desire to escape. The cause of alcoholism and drug addiction is negative and destructive thinking. The*

*cure is to think of freedom, sobriety,*
*and perfection, and to feel the*
*thrill of accomplishment."*

~Dr. Joseph Murphy

## Food for Thought

What is the importance of having "clean up conversations?"

# Guided Chakra Meditation Exercise

The following is a guided meditation exercise for connecting you to the energy of your Chakras. Here is a chart with the corresponding color and location for each Chakra. This exercise will allow you to begin to silence the internal chatter within.

Breathe...Breathe...Breathe. Practice silencing your mind at least three times a day. Do this for a minimum of at least five minutes each time. The longer you can maintain your meditative state, the better. (Do not do this with eyes closed while driving or operating machinery.) The Chakras ascend up along the spinal column and exit the body through the top of the head as follows:

The first Chakra is the Earth Chakra and is located at the bottom of our feet. The color is brown.

The second Chakra is the Root Chakra. It is located near the anus and runs down to our feet its color is red.

The third Chakra is the Sacral Chakra. It is located in the groin or genital area of the body and its color is orange.

The fourth Chakra is the Solar Plexus Chakra. It is located just above your navel or bellybutton and its color is yellow.

The fifth Chakra is the Heart Chakra. It is located in the middle of your chest and its color is green.

The sixth Chakra is the Higher Heart Chakra just above your breast. The color is pink.

The seventh Chakra is your Throat Chakra. It is located at the base of your neck at your collarbone and its color is blue.

The eighth Chakra is your Third Eye Chakra. It is located in the middle of your forehead between your eyes and its color is indigo.

The ninth Chakra is your Crown Chakra. It is located at the top of your head and its color is violet or purple.

The tenth Chakra is your Higher Crown Chakra it is located just above your head. The color is white

# Chakra Meditation: Step by Step Directions:

*1. With each exhale let go.*

*2. Surrender and release all thoughts from the past and all concerns for the future.*

*3. Be still and know that you are a child of God.*

*4. Let the stillness take you on a wondrous journey through the Chakras.*

*5. Breathe deep into each of your Chakras, for this is where the Universal Mind lives.*

*6. Stand in whichever color and bodily location you are called to and breathe deeply into that area.*

*7. Surround yourself in the color corresponding to the Chakra you are focusing on.*

*8. Begin to listen for and hear what emerges.*

*9. Look at the area of your life in which you desire a real*

*breakthrough and then surrender.*

Remember, there is no right or wrong way to do this meditation. You are unique and your body will respond in a way that is perfect for you. Even if you feel nothing at first, know that energetically you are preparing your body to receive a higher level of energy directly from Source. Many people experience a feeling of aliveness and energy flow almost immediately. If you don't feel a boost in your energy level right away, do not despair, you will come to it with practice. By your efforts and actions you are laying the groundwork to receive this energetic tune up and will surely reap the benefits. This is how the Chakra System works!

# Foundation Five

# Prayer-The Sacred Language Of The Soul

In prayer, you become still and centered. When you pray you retreat into the sacred silence within, and you are praying for yourself or others. You don't need a special place or specific words; you can go into your closet and pray just as Jesus has instructed us. Prayer is communion with the Creator, and you pray from an attitude of gratitude and reverence for all life. When you learn to become fluent in prayer it becomes the sacred language of your soul, you will pray with ease—as naturally as you breathe. Stilling your thoughts and being fully attuned to the presence of The Divine you become a special conduit of prayer. When your prayer practice is more about being than about doing, then all of life becomes a prayer. Take on prayer first thing in the morning as soon as you awake. Do this even before you get out of the bed. Get present as you lay in the bed, say to yourself, "All my needs are met...I am getting better and better every day... Thank you for another day." You might say something like, "Divine Intelligence, guide my thoughts today," then ask for what you truly desire. Ask for it in a positive, direct and clear manner, then be still and wait on the power of your prayers to deliver your next action. Always remember to pray for others as you would for yourself.

## Four Kinds of Prayer:

1. *Prayers for the World Without (material benefits and help)*

2. *Prayers for the World Within (virtues, grace and healing)*

3. *Prayers for Others—prayer treatments and services*

4. *Prayers for Illumination and gaining an understanding of who we are at a much higher level. As well as establishing our relationship with the Source of our lives.*

The first three types of prayer have their roots in feeling and desire. The fourth type of prayer brings us to the point where prayer ends and meditation can begin.

# The Law Of What You Sow; So Shall You Reap

What you sow, so shall you reap. Some call this Karma. You plant something and that which you planted will grow sooner or later. What goes around comes around. You put something out there it will come back sooner or later. These are laws that are 100% true. If you swim in a sea of dis-empowered thoughts, disparage everyone and everything then that is exactly what will be returned to you. A barrage of negative, hateful and upsetting events will overwhelm you, leaving you in a place of despair. Live in the World Without and all that the outside world had to offer becomes available to you. Remember you were meant to live your life from the World Within. It is our ego that lives in the world without.

Do not hate anything, not even the things you consider bad, wrong or hurtful. By planting negative seeds you sow poisonous vines that entrap, entangle and essentially choke the life right out of you. Hate creates friction in every area of life, and allows for health problems that inhibit your growth. Hate also fosters relationships that are incompatible and can also cause your career to fail. Hating is like you, taking the poison expecting the other person to die. If you are not having hateful or upsetting, angry or pissed off, mad or just plain negative thoughts, then what kind of thoughts are you having? Are they producing the results you desire? Remember, you get to choose, all the time!

*"Let go or be dragged."*
~ Zen Proverb

When you do housework it is important to really clean up thoroughly. Self-discipline is like cleaning up. And when you take on self-discipline, it is the time to take on self-discipline fully. You cannot take it on at 75% or 87% or even 98%, you must be 100% fully committed. Maybe you do the big clean up once a year or seasonally. You get into the corners, and the nooks and crannies; you clean the oven, under the rug and even organize your junk drawer. You remove all the stuff that has been accumulating over weeks, months or years, and give the house a thorough cleaning. Remember it is discipline not desire that determines your destiny. In your emotional and spiritual life more often than not, you have let stuff build up. You have a low operating level of integrity and self–

discipline. You handle the most urgent issues and let the less significant irritations fester in the corners of your mind.

If your money begins to get short you go to work on getting more money right away. If you are having a health issue you can't get to the doctor's office, pharmacy or holistic healer quick enough. On the other side, if someone hurts your feelings you suck it up or hold it deep inside rather than getting it handled right away. You might even add a bit of drama to it or create a story about whatever it is that has happened and use that as the excuse to not communicate the problem. These types of issues need to be cleaned up as soon as possible. If they are not handled sooner they will affect you later. It is times like these that we have to really be self-disciplined and operate with a higher level of integrity. You must clean your entire house. You have to clear out all the baggage from the past you have been holding on to for dear life. The more you release and surrender the more space to create all that you really desire.

Then you must get into every little crack and find forgiveness. You must find forgiveness for yourself first, and then forgiveness for others. No one is making you wrong, other than you, so stop invalidating your actions. Let go and go within, and you will be rewarded for your actions.

What are the areas of life are you dealing with now where you can clean up, let go, surrender and release the negative seeds you have sown? Look for the opportunity to ask for forgiveness and then accept it with your whole heart. Remember you are creating an open space to create from. Forgiveness gives us the space to create. This is all about clearing a space created from living with a high level of integrity, self-discipline, forgiveness and love.

The light of dawn signifies a new day. When you awaken refreshed in body and spirit, you are connected and at one with Source. You are attentive to divine ideas and guidance. Be grateful, as you are standing in the presence of gratitude. Know that all your needs are met and everything really is perfect. Allow your Genius that Lives Within out, to give you the life of your dreams. Take on all that you have learned from this book and practice it, it works!

## Question to Ponder:

What control do you have over the Law of Karma?

Sowing and reaping means giving and getting, planting and growing. In other words, this law is also the return of what we put out coming back to us.

# Visualization Begins
# The Manifestation Process

Most of us are not willing to work very hard. Once you have begun the process of seeing what you want, you must hold it as *having been* successful, and having achieved the desired results. You must literally see the end of the process first, by seeing yourself receive the outcome you desire. See all that it will require to achieve your most wanted results and go for it. Seeing the finished product before you take a step in the direction of your dreams is vital. It is as if you have tilled the soil, planted the seeds, and before you plant the seeds you have a very good idea of what the crop will yield. See it, this is visualization. At first it may not be very clear or organized, as you practice this daily it will begin to take form and soon blossom. It is going to take hard work, practice and self-discipline

Visualization begins the manifestation process. As you see the picture coming together, the habits and resources needed to create your vision will show up. One thought will lead to another and soon your thoughts will give you the actions to take. The various actions you take, give you each and every next step to take. As you practice this you will also begin to understand that the world must have been thought into existence before it became the world. You are just practicing the same method employed by the Creator. Remember, this same method of creation also always works through us.

A writer sees his story before he begins and then it gets created, and an inventor visualizes his invention in pretty much the same way. The sculptor sees his finished work of art as complete when he looks at a cube of uncut marble. He simply has to remove everything that is not a part of what he sees as the finished work. As Michelangelo was to have said, "David was already there; I just removed all that was not David." As you practice this process you will deepen and develop faith in your vision. What I mean by faith is "The substance of things hoped for, the evidence of things not seen." With self-discipline you will develop the confidence which allows you to concentrate. As you practice concentrating on that which you desire, you'll begin to exclude thoughts that keep you from achieving that which you want. The longer you can hold the image of what you desire, the greater will be your ability to manifest your desires.

# Visualization And Meditation

## This meditation is creative

*Allow yourself to relax deeply:*

*During this meditation, I would like you to not only be still in your body, inhibit all thoughts to the very best of your ability and relax. Let go. Let the muscles all over your body relax and take their relaxed state; this will remove all pressure from your nerves and eliminate tension which so frequently produces physical exhaustion and makes it very difficult to meditate.*

*Relax breathe, breathe, breathe take at least three deep breaths.*

*Now create and envision a wall in front of you.*

*See a blank wall 5 feet in front of you. Make it a beige colored wall with no texture just a blank wall.*

*Now create a black dot on the wall. Imagine you have a black marker and you draw a black dot on the wall about the size of a quarter.*

*Can you see it? Keep looking until you can see it.*

*Now create three dots about six inches in front of your nose. Make one at the height of the top of your head. Then make one at your right shoulder and the third one at your left shoulder. Make a triangle with three black dots six inches in front of your face. Can you see it? See it.*

*Now create three long black lines and connect the three dots that are six inches away and in the shape of a triangle to the one dot on the blank wall five feet in front of you. Can you see the object you just created? Can you see it? See it.*

*What do you see? What did you create?*

*You created a prism. Now create the sun shining through the prism, see a rainbow coming out of the other side of the prism. See colors...Red, Orange, Yellow, Green, Blue, Indigo and Violet...breathe, breathe, and breathe.*

*On the count of three have it all disappear.*

*Now create a blank brick wall in front of you and turn it into a door, any type of door you like. A steel door, stained glass, wooden or screen door. It could be a double door or an office door. Any type of door you wish. See it? See it.*

*Open the door.*

*Step through the door...create your world. Create a world you love. A place you really enjoy, or enjoyed. Create your dream place. Lawn, mountains, city streets, deck, steps, rocks, meadow, lake, waterfall create whatever you choose. Create your world and get comfortable in it.*

*Then look a distance away from where you are sitting or standing or laying and see a box, bag or case. When you open the case you will find something that thing will be very important to you. Look and listen for that still small voice.*

*Sit in the silence for five minutes minimum.*

*Now take a nice panoramic look around your space then get up and walk slowly back to your door.*

*Walk back to your door open it and leave your space behind you.*

*Once you our outside of your world close the door. Breathe, breathe, and breathe.*

*Shake your hands, yawn and slowly open your eyes and you bring yourself back into the room.*

## Take out your journal and answer the following questions:

- What did your door look like?

- What was your world like?

- What did your bag, box or case look like?

- What was in it?

- What did you hear?

Notice: **YOU MADE IT ALL UP.** Yes you created the world you love. You have the power and ability to create anything that you are willing to think about and take action on. You now begin to realize just how much is within your control. You have the ability to create to your hearts' desire.

It is said that, "you cannot make a silk purse from a sow's ear." It is very important that you learn to clear away all the thoughts that are not aligned with what you desire. They will only get in your way. You must create a mental image of what you desire. In your mind's eye, design your dreams hold on to them with faith and a strong desire to receive them. As you practice with strong faith and a strong desire for what you want, that which you yearn for will manifest. Many have taken this on and succeeded and then there are others who just don't have any luck at producing the results or fulfilling on the law. What is keeping them from the fulfillment of that which they desire? Their attention is on power, wealth and good health. These are the things of the World Without. The people who are not producing results are putting their energy on the *effects*, rather than the *cause*. Re-member we can only receive the *effects* once the *cause* is clear.

Be in the world and not of the world. We miss the mark when we are caught up in the world. We hit the mark when we come from the World Within. A man concentrating on the fact that he is not producing results produces no results. A woman talking about why things cannot happen cannot produce results. A girl being told there is not enough money, time or energy, will have little money, time or energy. As you continue to concentrate on lack, you create poverty. As you concentrate on sickness, you create disease. As you hold on to not being good enough, you'll never become good enough. So what works, what will have us fulfill on the Law? The answer is simple; putting your attention on that which you desire and not on the things you do not want. Put your eye on the prize, the result, or the outcome you wish to achieve. This is a very powerful law that works to perfection every time. If the law works to create sickness, deficiency, inadequacy and fear, then you can count on it to create courage, wealth, health and great loving relationships.

When we allow ourselves to practice going within, our Sub-Conscience or Divine Mind can run the show. The law does not work when we are worried or fearful. Take for instance, the story of the mom who has her little child help her plant a vegetable garden. The next day when mom is preparing lunch the little guy is out in the garden digging up the seeds to see if they are carrots, peas and watermelon yet. As adults know we have to let nature take its course when it comes to growing the garden. It takes the sun, water and time for the plants to germinate and sprout. When it comes to us we have to sow our seeds, which are our desires, wishes and requests and leave them undisturbed. Please do not think this means don't take any action on that which you desire. This means be still and be ready to move in the direction that your thoughts guide you to move in. Re-member your thoughts create your word and your words create your world.

## Thoughts to Ponder:

Is it time to clean up and remove old worn out ways you have been thinking and being?

What seeds you have been sowing? Remember you get to choose how your life goes.

The Genius Lives Within is your guide to direct and inspire you to success.

# Peace: The Voice of Stillness

When you are seeking guidance, sometimes you need a nudge in the right direction. Sometimes, you may feel lost, or have no idea where to go and how to get there. However great the need, look for guidance by setting aside distracting activities and quieting your thoughts. As you move into the stillness and allow your attention to turn inward, focus on your breath. Tell yourself, "I am calm and I am receptive." Listen through your Divine Intelligence and be guided. In the still and open space of possibilities, listen. If your mind races, calm it by becoming aware of your breathing and being confident as you move forward.

*"When I get quiet and listen, God fills my mind with divine ideas, informs my thoughts, leads me to right action, and encourages me on my life's journey. Through prayer and meditation, I tap into the wisdom of God and find the answers I seek."* ~ Unity

Remember earlier when we spoke about laws? What are some of those laws? Gravity is a law; everything in existence has an opposite. Our words create our world. This is also a law. The use of mental images to create is using a law. We call this law visualization. It is the practice of making mental images and then bringing the images into reality. Said another way, it is the ability to create a model or blueprint from which you can bring forth your future. It's very important to make your model or blueprint clear and simple without fear. You must create it to suit your heart's desire. Fear is man's greatest enemy and it is behind every failure, sickness and bad human relationship. Love casts out all fear. Love is an emotional attachment to the good things of life. Fall in love with hard work. Fall in love with living your life at a high level of integrity, and create habits that are worth having. Become self-disciplined and live in the blissful anticipation of the best of all outcomes and sure enough it will materialize.

> *"Be still, and know that I am God!"*
> ~Psalm 46:10

Remember, the only limitations that can be placed upon you, are those you place upon yourself. In the World Within, there are no limitations. The Universe is the limit and you have an unlimited supply of creative energy to pull from. Ask your Divine Sub Conscience to support you in your creations.

You must create it in your Sub Conscience, in your imagination first. It must show up in the World Within, before it can manifest in the World Without. Where your heart is, so is your treasure. It really takes something on your part to make this happen. You must be self-disciplined and operate with a high level of integrity. You must be committed to make things happen.

Meditate three times a day every day for at least ten to twenty minutes. When you meditate you are learning to quiet the chatter from the World Without that you are hearing in your head. As you learn to sit in the silence you will begin to hear that still small voice, the voice within your subconscious. All your needs are met, and you are getting better and better every day. What you are practicing really does strengthen your connection to the Divine within.

# Food for Thought:

What happens when you sit in the stillness?

# No Time Like The Present

In remembering the hallmarks of the Genius Lives Within, let's review them briefly so that you can keep them in the forefront of your mind. As you practice them over and over again, they gradually become a part of you. I've outlined a few of the foundations for you to be mindful of as you choose this new direction for your life

Thoughts create our words. Words create our world. Words come from within. Power comes from within. You cannot display powers that you don't have. You must become aware or conscious of your power. You can never become mindful of your power until you learn that all power is from within.

- The Laws, what are the laws that if you learn them and practice them you can achieve anything you desire?

- Every thought is cause, every condition is an effect. You must learn to control your thoughts so as to

CREATE what you desire.

- All power is from within and under your control, the Genius Lives Within.

- The Omnipotent Law, Source is the basis of it all. The Divine is the Law.

- The World Within makes, creates, and gives us the World Without. Here are some of the manifestations of this law: Up/down; in/out; good/bad; right/wrong; success/ failure; empowered/dis-empowered; should/choice; abun-dance/lack; health/sickness; the World Within/the World Without and so on and so forth.

- Remember the World Within is creative and everything you find without has been created by it.

- Your thoughts create your words, your words create your world, and your world gives you your life

- The World Without is a reflection of the World Within. It is a mirror and our thoughts determine our present and future life.

- A sacred place for us to be is in the presence of the Universal Mind, The Divine, the Omnipotent; God.

- As you become present to the now, you can put the past in the past and focus on creating the future you desire.

- The Law of Visualization: You create from your thoughts, and if you can visualize it, then you can make it happen.

- All you have to do is say what it is you desire. "Anything you ask for in my name I shall give to you…"

- The Law of Karma or what you sow, so shall you reap. As we said it as children, "what goes around comes around."

- Meditation is the act of going into that still, quiet place where we can attain balance, inner peace and calmness.

Be still and know that you are God. All thought comes from within. To receive the answers you are requesting you must be quiet. It is in the stillness and quiet that the mind becomes tranquil, and like a still clear lake, it can reflect the divine images of peace and perfection. From these reflections, you can create the incredible future of your dreams. What comes next is totally up to you. In the pages of this little book you have been given instructions that allow you to take your life to the next level. If you do the work of honoring your Spirit and acknowledging your Genius within, you will witness the most miraculous trans-formation ever seen before, and it will be you.

> *"Anything you ask for in my name I shall give to you…" John 14: 13-14*

> *"Ask and it shall be given you, seek, and you shall find, knock and the door will be opened…" Matthew 7:7*

# Journal Exercise

Write in your journal in your own handwriting. Write your thoughts on what it is you truly desire. Do not use a computer or a typewriter for this exercise. There is a different type of think-ing taking place when you type using a keyboard. Writing by hand allows for a natural flow of ideas. Write down what comes to you immediately after your meditation, or upon waking in the morning. Keep it clear and simple; bold statements and clear short phrases. Stay away from creating a story or a big drama for these statements. Here are some examples below. Remember there are no limits. This is your life you are creating, so have fun and be creative.

1. Success is mine.

2. I love my life unabashedly.

3. I always finish what I start.

4. I have compassion for myself and others.

5. Thoughtfulness and prosperity give me my being-ness.

6. I can only control myself.

7. I get to say how my life goes.

8. All my needs are met.

9. My words create my world and my world is magical.

10. I honor my Spirit!

# Final Words

You are in the process of remembering that thought is creative, and that thought is the activity behind all constructive endeavors. When you think about it, what is more valuable than your thoughts? Creating with your thoughts takes attention, discipline and operating with a high level of integrity. By giving your thoughts your full attention, you develop your concentration and focus. The more you concentrate, the more you develop your spiritual abilities; the mightiest force of all. You are the only thinker in your Universe. This is the art of all art, the science of all science, the supreme knowledge gleaned from the mystery schools of spiritual wisdom. To take on this practice completely takes work. It takes effort, discipline and a high level of integrity. It also takes time and it takes practice; lots of practice. Allow this instruction to become a labor of love as you gain greater access to the Genius that Lives Within! I promise you, the results you will produce are worth it!

# ABOUT THE AUTHOR

Margaret C Pazant is a world renowned motivational keynote speaker and transformational life coach. She has impacted the lives of thousands and thousands of people all over the world for the last twenty years. She has taken on becoming masterful in the knowledge of many religions, philosophies and New Thought technologies. Growing up in New York City with her two sisters and brother she had the wonderful opportunity of experiencing the spiritual practices of a culturally diverse community.

Margaret grew up in a Methodist/Baptist household going to Sunday school and singing in the children's choir. She attended Friday night services at the Synagogue with her class mates. As well as Saturday morning confession at the local Catholic church with friends. When Margaret attended chanting at the Cathedral of St. John the Divine with Hilda in the seventies a new world of spirituality came into her consciousness. After extensive training and development with Landmark Education Corporation and becoming a Landmark Forum Leader as well as a senior consultant for Vanto Group for many years, Margaret went on a personal journey to discover the Genius Lives Within. She has designed and delivers a nine session coaching series to complement the book *Genius Lives Within: Accessing Our Birthright Power*. Ms. Pazant currently resides in Los Angeles, California and has one daughter and seven beautiful grandchildren.

**Margaret C. Pazant**
Is available for
**Speaking Engagements**
**Coaching for Coaches**
**Personal, One on One and Group Coaching**
**She also offers Coaching Programs and Series**
**as well as Coaches Trainings**

**Contact her at**
**P.O. Box 561453**
**Los Angeles, CA 900056**
**Margaretpazant.com**
**Marpazant@gmail.com**